Mother Goose's Melodies

A Platt & Munk **ALL ABOARD BOOK**™

Mother

Goose's Melodies

Illustrated by Cristina Ong

PLATT & MUNK, PUBLISHERS

Copyright © 1987 by Platt & Munk, Publishers. Illustrations copyright © 1987 by Cristina Ong. All rights reserved.
Platt & Munk, Publishers is a division of Grosset & Dunlap, which is a member of The Putnam Publishing Group, New York.
ALL ABOARD BOOKS is a trademark of The Putnam Publishing Group. Published simultaneously in Canada. Printed
in the U.S.A. Library of Congress Catalog Card Number: 86-63967   ISBN 0-448-34303-7   A B C D E F G H I J

SING A SONG OF SIXPENCE

Sing a song of sixpence,
A pocket full of rye;
Four and twenty blackbirds
Baked in a pie.

When the pie was opened,
The birds began to sing;
Wasn't that a dainty dish
To set before a king?

The king was in his counting-house,
Counting out his money;
The queen was in the parlor,
Eating bread and honey.

The maid was in the garden,
Hanging out the clothes;
When down came a blackbird
And pecked off her nose.

THREE BLIND MICE

Three blind mice, see how they run!
They all ran after the farmer's wife,
Who cut off their tails with a carving knife,
Did you ever see such a sight in your life,
As three blind mice?

MY LITTLE DOG

Oh where, oh where has my little dog gone?
Oh where, oh where can he be?
With his ears cut short and his tail cut long,
Oh where, oh where is he?

THIS LITTLE PIG

This little pig went to market,
This little pig stayed home,
This little pig had roast beef,
This little pig had none,
And this little pig cried,
"Wee-wee-wee-wee-wee,"
All the way home.

POLLY

Polly put the kettle on,
Polly put the kettle on,
Polly put the kettle on,
We'll all have tea.

Sukey take it off again,
Sukey take it off again,
Sukey take it off again,
They've all gone away.

JACK SPRAT

Jack Sprat could eat no fat,
His wife could eat no lean;
And so, betwixt them both, you see,
They licked the platter clean.

LITTLE JACK HORNER

Little Jack Horner
Sat in the corner,
Eating his Christmas pie;
He put in his thumb,
And pulled out a plum,
And said, "What a good boy am I!"

PAT-A-CAKE

Pat-a-cake, pat-a-cake, baker's man,
Bake me a cake as fast as you can;
Pat it and prick it, and mark it with T,
Put it in the oven for Tommy and me.

MARY HAD A LITTLE LAMB

Mary had a little lamb,
Its fleece was white as snow;
And everywhere that Mary went
The lamb was sure to go.

It followed her to school one day,
Which was against the rule;
It made the children laugh and play
To see a lamb in school.

And so the teacher turned it out,
But still it lingered near,
And waited patiently about
Till Mary did appear.

"Why does the lamb love Mary so?"
The eager children cry;
"Why, Mary loves the lamb, you know,"
The teacher did reply.

LONDON BRIDGE

London Bridge is falling down,
Falling down, falling down,
London Bridge is falling down,
My fair lady.

Build it up with wood and clay,
Wood and clay, wood and clay,
Build it up with wood and clay,
My fair lady.

RING-A-RING O' ROSES

Ring-a-ring o' roses,
A pocket full of posies,
A-tishoo! A-tishoo!
We all fall down.

The cows are in the meadow,
Lying fast asleep,
A-tishoo! A-tishoo!
We all get up again.

JACK AND JILL

Jack and Jill
Went up the hill,
To fetch a pail of water;
Jack fell down,
And broke his crown,
And Jill came tumbling after.

PETER PIPER

Peter Piper picked a peck of pickled
  peppers;
A peck of pickled peppers Peter Piper
  picked.
If Peter Piper picked a peck of
  pickled peppers,
Where's the peck of pickled peppers
  Peter Piper picked?

IT'S RAINING

It's raining, it's pouring,
The old man is snoring;
He went to bed
With a cold in his head,
And couldn't get up in the morning.

EENSEY WEENSEY SPIDER

Eensey Weensey spider climbed up the water spout,
Down came the rain and washed the spider out,
Out came the sun and dried up all the rain,
Eensey Weensey spider climbed up the spout again.

LITTLE BOY BLUE

Little Boy Blue,
Come blow your horn,
The sheep's in the meadow,
The cow's in the corn.
Where is the boy
Who looks after the sheep?
He's under a haystack
Fast asleep.
Will you wake him?
No, not I,
For if I do,
He's sure to cry.

DIDDLETY, DIDDLETY, DUMPTY

Diddlety, diddlety, dumpty,
The cat ran up the plum tree;
Half a crown
To fetch her down,
Diddlety, diddlety, dumpty.

POP GOES THE WEASEL

Up and down the City Road,
In and out the Eagle,
That's the way the money goes,
Pop goes the weasel!

Half a pound of tuppenny rice,
Half a pound of treacle,
Mix it up and make it nice,
Pop goes the weasel!

YANKEE DOODLE

Yankee Doodle came to town,
Riding on a pony;
He stuck a feather in his cap
And called it macaroni.

HEY DIDDLE DIDDLE

Hey diddle diddle,
The cat and the fiddle,
The cow jumped over the moon;
The little dog laughed
To see such sport,
And the dish ran away with the spoon.

RIDE A COCK-HORSE

Ride a cock-horse to Banbury Cross,
To see a fine lady upon a white horse;
Rings on her fingers and bells on her toes,
She shall have music wherever she goes.

BAGPIPES

Puss came dancing out of a barn
With a pair of bagpipes under her arm;
She could sing nothing but, Fiddle cum fee,
The mouse has married the humble-bee.
Pipe, cat—dance, mouse—
We'll have a wedding at our fine house.

1, 2

3, 4

5, 6

7, 8

9, 10

ONE, TWO

1, 2,
Buckle my shoe;

3, 4,
Knock at the door;

5, 6,
Pick up sticks;

7, 8,
Lay them straight;

9, 10,
A big fat hen;

11, 12,
Dig and delve;

13, 14,
Maids a-courting;

15, 16,
Maids in the kitchen;

17, 18,
Maids in waiting;

19, 20,
My plate's empty.

BAA, BAA, BLACK SHEEP

Baa, baa, black sheep
Have you any wool?
Yes sir, yes sir,
Three bags full;
One for the master,
And one for the dame,
And one for the little boy
Who lives down the lane.

HIGGLETY, PIGGLETY

Higglety, pigglety, pop!
The dog has eaten the mop;
The pig's in a hurry,
The cat's in a flurry,
Higglety, pigglety, pop!

OH DEAR, WHAT CAN THE MATTER BE?

Oh dear, what can the matter be?
Dear, dear, what can the matter be?
Oh dear, what can the matter be?
Johnny's so long at the fair.

He promised he'd buy me a fairing
   should please me,
And then for a kiss, oh! he vowed
   he would tease me,
He promised he'd bring me
   a bunch of blue ribbons
To tie up my bonny brown hair.

BLIND MAN'S BUFF

Blind man, blind man,
Sure you can't see?
Turn round three times,
And try to catch me.
Turn east, turn west,
Catch as you can,
Did you think you'd caught me?
Blind, blind man!

PIT, PAT

Pit, pat, well-a-day,
Little Robin flew away;
Where can little Robin be?
Gone into the cherry tree.

MARY'S PRETTY BIRD

Mary had a pretty bird,
Feathers bright and yellow,
Slender legs—upon my word,
He was a pretty fellow!

The sweetest note he'd always sung,
Which much delighted Mary,
She often, when the cage was hung,
Sat hearing her canary.

HERE WE GO ROUND

Here we go round the mulberry bush,
The mulberry bush, the mulberry bush,
Here we go round the mulberry bush,
On a cold and frosty morning.

This is the way we wash our hands,
Wash our hands, wash our hands,
This is the way we wash our hands,
On a cold and frosty morning.

This is the way we wash our clothes,
Wash our clothes, wash our clothes,
This is the way we wash our clothes,
On a cold and frosty morning.

This is the way we go to school,
Go to school, go to school,
This is the way we go to school,
On a cold and frosty morning.

OLD KING COLE

Old King Cole
Was a merry old soul,
And a merry old soul was he;
He called for his pipe,
And he called for his bowl,
And he called for his fiddlers three.

Every fiddler he had a fiddle,
And a very fine fiddle had he;
Oh, there's none so rare
As can compare
With King Cole and his fiddlers three.

JACK

Jack be nimble,
Jack be quick,
Jack jump over
The candlestick.

A LONG SONG

As I was going along, long, long,
A-singing a comical song, song, song,
The lane that I went was so long, long, long,
And the song that I sang was so long, long, long,
And so I went singing along!